D1526376

A Gift for:

_____

From:

_____

ZONDERVAN®

The Creeds

© 2014 by Zondervan

Requests for information should be addressed to:
Zondervan, Grand Rapids, Michigan 49530

ISBN-13: 978-0-310-34338-7

Cover design: Micah Kandros

Interior Photography: © Shutterstock 1–8, 10–13, 15–17, 19–22, 24–25, 27–31, 33–37, 39–42, 44–46, 49–54, 57–62, 64–70, 73–77, 79–84, 86–89, 91–95, 97–101, 103–104, 106–111, 113–114, 116–117, 119–123, 125–126, 128–132, 135–138, 141–146, 149–150, 152–153, 155–158, 160

Interior design: Mallory Perkins

Printed in China

14 15 16 17 18 19 20 /TIMS/ 22 21 20 19 18 17 16 15 14 13 12 11 10 9 8 7 6 5 4 3 2 1

THE
CREEDS

REFLECTIONS AND SCRIPTURE ON THE
APOSTLES' AND NICENE CREEDS

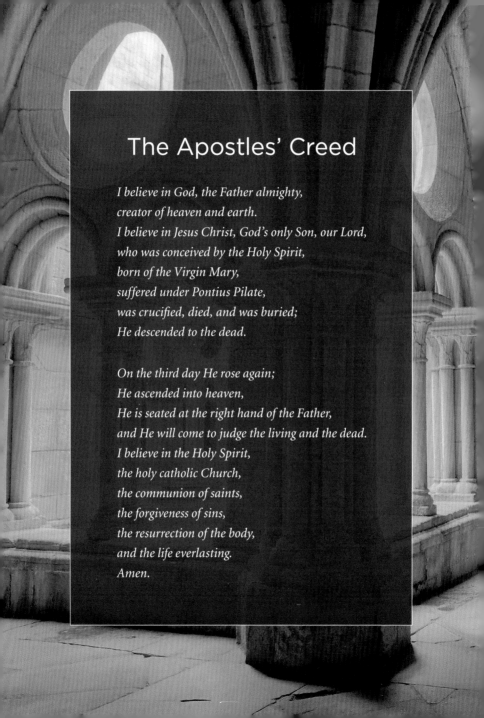

The Apostles' Creed

I believe in God, the Father almighty,
creator of heaven and earth.
I believe in Jesus Christ, God's only Son, our Lord,
who was conceived by the Holy Spirit,
born of the Virgin Mary,
suffered under Pontius Pilate,
was crucified, died, and was buried;
He descended to the dead.

On the third day He rose again;
He ascended into heaven,
He is seated at the right hand of the Father,
and He will come to judge the living and the dead.
I believe in the Holy Spirit,
the holy catholic Church,
the communion of saints,
the forgiveness of sins,
the resurrection of the body,
and the life everlasting.
Amen.

"What could be more foolish
than to think that all this rare
fabric of heaven and earth
could come by chance?"
—Anatole France

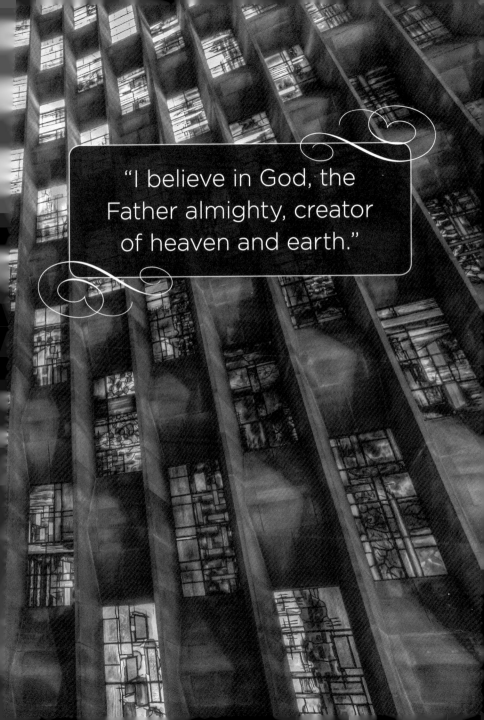

"I believe in God, the Father almighty, creator of heaven and earth."

*S*eeing the great wonders of creation, getting up close to a towering, snow-capped mountain, or looking up into the Milky Way on a clear night away from the city may make us feel very small—or even insignificant. But the same Bible that declares Him to be mighty beyond imagining also proclaims His Father's heart . . . and tender care.

> *"He alone stretches out the heavens*
> *and treads on the waves of the sea.*
> *He is the Maker of the Bear and Orion,*
> *the Pleiades and the constellations of the south.*
> *He performs wonders that cannot be fathomed,*
> *miracles that cannot be counted."*
>
> —Job 9:8–10

Come, let us bow down in worship,
let us kneel before the LORD our Maker;
for he is our God
and we are the people of his pasture,
the flock under his care.

—PSALM 95:6–7

"I would rather be what God chose to make me than the most glorious creature that I could think of; for to have been thought about, born in God's thought, and then made by God, is the dearest, grandest and most precious thing in all thinking."

—GEORGE MACDONALD

No one knows better than our Creator how needy we are and how utterly lost our lives are apart from Him.

GOD, your Redeemer,
who shaped your life in your mother's womb, says:
"I am GOD. I made all that is.
With no help from you I spread out the skies
and laid out the earth."

—ISAIAH 44:24 MSG

The LORD is like a father to his children,
tender and compassionate to those who fear him.
For he knows how weak we are;
he remembers we are only dust.

—PSALM 103:13–14 NLT

"Before me, even as behind, God is, and all is well."
—John Greenleaf Whittier

All that is truly good in our lives—light, color, beauty, wonder, and love—flows from God Himself. He is the Source and Headwaters of everything worthy and worthwhile that we will ever encounter.

"You've forgotten me, God, who made you,
who unfurled the skies, who founded the earth."
—Isaiah 51:13 MSG

"We know that God is everywhere; but certainly
we feel His presence most when His works are on
the grandest scale spread before us; and it is in the
unclouded night-sky, where His worlds wheel their
silent course, that we read clearest His infinitude,
His omnipotence, His omnipresence."
—Charlotte Brontë

Every good and perfect gift is from above,
coming down from the Father of the heavenly lights,
who does not change like shifting shadows.
—James 1:17

God's handiwork extends to the outer edges of all that is or could be . . . and yet He is near enough to hear and respond to a wordless cry from the weakest and most overwhelmed of His sons and daughters.

I lift up my eyes to the mountains—
where does my help come from?
My help comes from the LORD,
the Maker of heaven and earth.

—PSALM 121:1–2

"All I have seen teaches me to trust the Creator
for all I have not seen."

—RALPH WALDO EMERSON

"Belief is a wise wager. Granted that faith cannot be
proved, what harm will come to you if you gamble
on its truth and it proves false? If you gain, you
gain all; if you lose, you lose nothing. Wager, then,
without hesitation, that He exists."

—BLAISE PASCAL

"There is not one blade of grass, there is no color in
this world that is not intended to make us rejoice."

—JOHN CALVIN

"All that I am I owe to Jesus Christ, revealed to me
in His divine Book."

—DAVID LIVINGSTONE

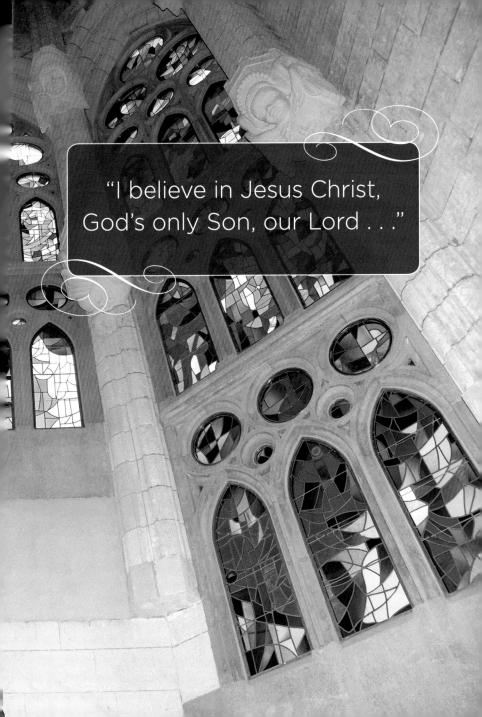

"I believe in Jesus Christ, God's only Son, our Lord . . ."

*W*hen He saw that nothing else would do, God entered this troubled world to bring help, hope, and salvation. He not only came to be with us, He also became one of us.

"But you, Bethlehem Ephrathah,
Though you are little among the thousands of Judah,
Yet out of you shall come forth to Me
The One to be Ruler in Israel,
Whose goings forth are from of old,
From everlasting."

—MICAH 5:2 NKJV

"In my vision at night I looked, and there before me was one like a son of man, coming with the clouds of heaven. He approached the Ancient of Days and was led into his presence. He was given authority, glory and sovereign power; all nations and peoples of every language worshiped him. His dominion is an everlasting dominion that will not pass away, and his kingdom is one that will never be destroyed."

—DANIEL 7:13–14

Jesus replied, "Don't you even yet know who I am, Philip, even after all this time I have been with you? Anyone who has seen me has seen the Father!"

—JOHN 14:9 TLB

To find a true and faithful friend is one of life's most valuable treasures—surpassing wealth and fame. Then to realize that the Son of God Himself is such a friend takes that wonder beyond comprehension.

"There is a God-shaped vacuum in the heart of every man which cannot be filled by any created thing, but only by God, the Creator, made known through Jesus Christ."

—Blaise Pascal

"Our Lord's message was Himself. . . . He did not come merely to give bread; He said, "I am the bread." He did not come merely to shed light; He said, "I am the light." He did not come merely to show the door; He said, "I am the door." He did not come merely to name a shepherd; He said, "I am the shepherd." He did not come merely to point the way; He said, "I am the way, the truth, and the life."

—J. Sidlow Baxter

"A rule I have had for years is: to treat the Lord
Jesus Christ as a personal friend. His is not a creed,
a mere doctrine, but it is He Himself that we have."

—D. L. Moody

The only Name that offers life beyond life and hope beyond hope
is still mocked, rejected, belittled, and disregarded to this very day.

"Jesus does not give recipes that show the way to God
as other teachers of religion do.
He is Himself the way."

—Karl Barth

"The dearest friend on earth is a mere shadow
compared to Jesus Christ."

—Oswald Chambers

For God so loved the world that he gave his one and only Son, that whoever believes in him shall not perish but have eternal life. For God did not send his Son into the world to condemn the world, but to save the world through him.

—JOHN 3:16–17

To have lived in the time and place of His first coming would have been glorious. But to live in daily anticipation of His second coming, knowing that at any moment He might appear in the clouds and call His church home, has a glory of its own.

"I saw this and fainted dead at his feet. His right hand
pulled me upright, his voice reassured me:
'Don't fear: I am First, I am Last, I'm Alive. I died, but I
came to life, and my life is now forever.'"

—REVELATION 1:16–18 MSG

"Christ, by highest heavens adored,
Christ the everlasting Lord!
Late in time behold him come,
Offspring of the virgin's womb.
Veiled in flesh the Godhead see;
Hail the incarnate Deity."

—CHARLES WESLEY

"Jesus Christ: the meeting place of eternity and time, the blending of deity and humanity, the junction of heaven and earth."

—Unknown Christian

"I know men and I tell you that Jesus Christ is no mere man. Between Him and every other person in the world there is no possible term of comparison. Alexander, Caesar, Charlemagne, and I have founded empires. But on what did we rest the creation of our genius? Upon force. Jesus Christ founded His empire upon love; and at this hour millions of men would die for Him."

—Napoleon

"... who was conceived by the Holy Spirit, born of the Virgin Mary ..."

*I*f we were to take away all of the traditions the world has attached to Christ's advent for the last two thousand years, its reality and its wonder would not be diminished.

> *"Our God, Jesus Christ, was, according to the*
> *appointment of God, conceived in the womb by*
> *Mary, of the seed of David,*
> *but by the Holy Spirit."*
>
> —Ignatius

> *"Therefore the LORD Himself will give you a sign:*
> *Behold, a virgin will be with child and bear a son, and she*
> *will call His name Immanuel."*
>
> —Isaiah 7:14 nasb

> "The cry of this world for meaning and hope and
> life was met one morning far away in the cry of
> a tiny babe. And with that cry, time stopped and
> started again. And it was new."
>
> —Unknown

> "Jesus Christ became Incarnate for one purpose, to
> make a way back to God that man might stand before
> Him as He was created to do, the friend and lover of
> God Himself."
>
> —Oswald Chambers

Think of it! The Ruler and Creator of the universe, entering His own creation as a helpless infant. No wonder so many angels wanted a corner of the night sky over Bethlehem to declare it!

"Those who assert that he was a mere man, begotten by Joseph . . . being ignorant of him who from the virgin is Emmanuel . . . are deprived of his gift, which is eternal life. Not receiving the incorruptible Word, they remain in mortal flesh and are debtors to death, not obtaining the antidote of life."

—IRENAEUS

"It was not suddenly and unannounced that Jesus came into a world that had been prepared for Him. The whole Old Testament is the story of a special preparation. . . . Only when all was ready, only in the fullness of His time, did Jesus come."

—PHILLIPS BROOKS

Mary asked the angel, "But how can I have a baby? I am a virgin." The angel replied, "The Holy Spirit shall come upon you, and the power of God shall overshadow you; so the baby born to you will be utterly holy—the Son of God."

—LUKE 1:34–35 TLB

The all-powerful Son of God made Himself vulnerable in order to bring strong help to those He loved. It's that way for every one of us. Stepping into another's world to bring encouragement and hope still makes us vulnerable to misunderstanding and rejection. And it is still worth the risk.

But when the fullness of time had come, God sent his Son, born of a woman.

—GALATIANS 4:4 NRSV

"O morning stars, together
Proclaim the holy birth!
And praises sing to God the King,
And peace to men on earth.
For Christ is born of Mary
And gathered all above,
While mortals sleep the angels keep
Their watch of wondering love."

—PHILLIPS BROOKS

"Rejoice, that the immortal God is born,
so that mortal man may live in eternity."

—JOHN HUSS

So the Word became human and made his home among us. He was full of unfailing love and faithfulness. And we have seen his glory, the glory of the Father's one and only Son.

—JOHN 1:14 NLT

Looking forward through the shadows of years yet to be, the Old Testament prophets saw the brightness of His coming. Today we look back on that brightness—and yet forward to a day brighter still, when He comes again.

"For a child has been born—for us!
the gift of a son—for us!
He'll take over
the running of the world.
His names will be: Amazing Counselor,
Strong God,
Eternal Father,
Prince of Wholeness.
His ruling authority will grow,
and there'll be no limits to the wholeness he brings."
—ISAIAH 9:6–7 MSG

"Now the virginity of Mary was hidden from the
prince of this world, as was also her offspring, and
the death of the Lord; three mysteries of renown,
which were wrought in silence by God."

—IGNATIUS

"The purpose and cause of the incarnation was that He
might illuminate the world by His wisdom
and excite it to the love of Himself."
—PETER ABELARD

"He was created of a mother whom He created.
He was carried by hands that He formed. He cried
in the manger in wordless infancy. He, the Word,
without whom all human eloquence is mute."

—AUGUSTINE

"He was Himself forsaken that none of His children
might ever need to utter His cry of loneliness."
—J. H. VINCENT

". . . suffered under Pontius Pilate, was crucified, died, and was buried; He descended to the dead."

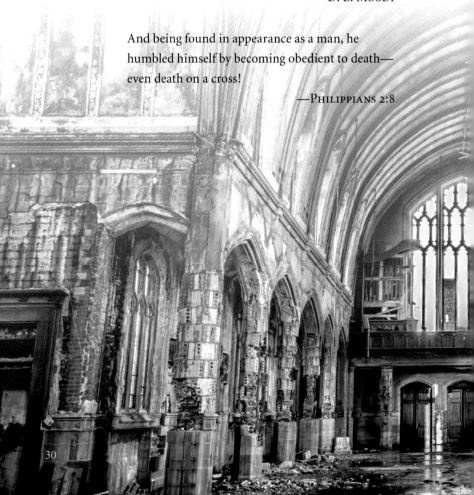

*T*here is no excuse, reason, or justification to carry shame that has already been carried on shoulders much wider than ours.

"My friends, there is one spot on earth where the fear of death, of sin, and of judgment need never trouble us, the only safe spot on earth where the sinner can stand—Calvary."

—D. L. Moody

And being found in appearance as a man, he humbled himself by becoming obedient to death—even death on a cross!

—Philippians 2:8

"Yet it was our grief he bore, our sorrows that weighed him down. And we thought his troubles were a punishment from God, for his own sins! But he was wounded and bruised for our sins. He was beaten that we might have peace; he was lashed—and we were healed!"

—Isaiah 53:4–5 TLB

"All other great men are valued for their lives; He, above all, for His death, around which mercy and truth, righteousness and peace, God and man are reconciled."

—Edward Thomson

The message of the cross seemed empty, irrelevant, and even foolish to many people in the first century. So it is in the twenty-first century. Yet for those who have embraced it, then and now, it has the same power to utterly restore and rebuild a human life.

> For the message of the cross is foolishness to those who are perishing, but to us who are being saved it is the power of God.
>
> —1 CORINTHIANS 1:18

> "Jesus died praying. His last words were words of prayer. The habit of life was strong in death. It may seem far off; but this event will come to us also. What will our last words be? Who can tell? But would it not be beautiful if our spirit were so steeped in the habit of prayer that the language of prayer came naturally to us at the last?"
>
> —JAMES STALKER

> ". . . just as Christian came up to the Cross, his burden loosed from off his shoulders, fell from off his back, and began to tumble down the hill, and so it continued to do till it came to the mouth of the sepulchre. There it fell in, and I saw it no more!"
>
> —JOHN BUNYAN, *The Pilgrim's Progress*

> As for me, God forbid that I should boast about anything except the cross of our Lord Jesus Christ. Because of that cross, my interest in all the attractive things of the world was killed long ago, and the world's interest in me is also long dead.
>
> —GALATIANS 6:14 TLB

The thick, heavy curtain in the temple was torn from top to bottom. It wasn't human hands tearing from the bottom, but divine hands tearing from the top, removing the barrier and opening access into God's presence, because of the price Jesus paid.

> Just then, as Pilate was sitting on the judgment seat, his wife sent him this message: "Leave that innocent man alone. I suffered through a terrible nightmare about him last night."
>
> —MATTHEW 27:19 NLT

> "Surely he was the Son of God!"
>
> —MATTHEW 27:54

And when Jesus had cried out again in a loud voice, he gave up his spirit. At that moment the curtain of the temple was torn in two from top to bottom. The earth shook, the rocks split and the tombs broke open. . . . When the centurion and those with him who were guarding Jesus saw the earthquake and all that had happened, they were terrified, and exclaimed, "Surely he was the Son of God!"

—MATTHEW 27:50-52, 54

"With a weak faith and a fearful heart, many a sinner stands before the Lord. It is not the strength of our faith, but the perfection of Christ's sacrifice that saves! No feebleness of faith, nor dimness of eye, no trembling of hand can change the efficacy of Christ's blood. The strength of our faith can add nothing to it, nor can the weakness of our faith take anything from Him. Faith (weak or strong) still reads the promise, 'the blood of Jesus Christ His Son cleanses us from all sin.'"

—HORATIUS BONAR

As He was dying on the cross, Jesus Christ cried out the word, *"Tetelestai!"* It is an accounting term that means "paid in full." With His death and by His blood, He paid the full price for all of our sins.

"What if thou hadst committed the sins of a thousand? What if thou hadst committed the sins of a million worlds? Christ's righteousness will cover, Christ's blood will cleanse thee from the guilt of all."

—George Whitefield

"God forsaken by God—who can understand it?"

—Martin Luther

You were dead because of your sins and because your sinful nature was not yet cut away. Then God made you alive with Christ, for he forgave all our sins. He canceled the record of the charges against us and took it away by nailing it to the cross.

—Colossians 2:13–14 NLT

"God took the worst thing that man could do to his Son, and transformed it into the best thing he could do for man."

—Unknown

"Death in vain forbids Him rise, Alleluia!
Christ has opened paradise, Alleluia!"

—Charles Wesley

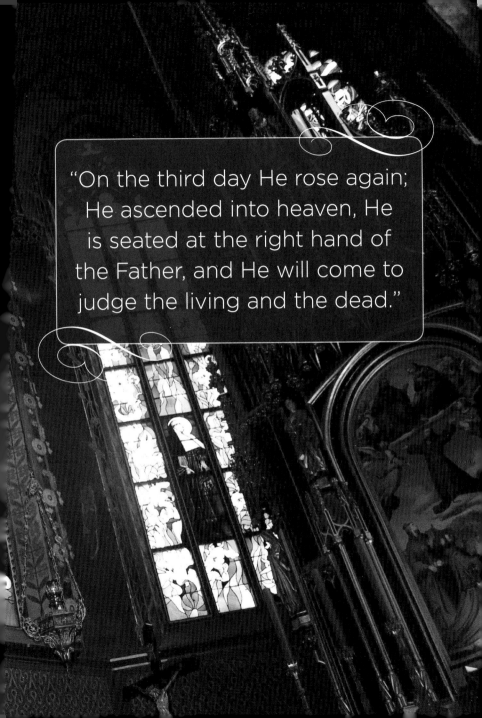

"On the third day He rose again; He ascended into heaven, He is seated at the right hand of the Father, and He will come to judge the living and the dead."

*B*ecause Jesus is alive, the shadow of death has been reduced to a simple doorway, with eternal life just over the threshold.

There was a violent earthquake, for an angel of the Lord came down from heaven and, going to the tomb, rolled back the stone and sat on it. His appearance was like lightning, and his clothes were white as snow. The guards were so afraid of him that they shook and became like dead men. The angel said to the women, "Do not be afraid, for I know that you are looking for Jesus, who was crucified. He is not here; he has risen, just as he said. Come and see the place where he lay. Then go quickly and tell his disciples: 'He has risen from the dead and is going ahead of you into Galilee. There you will see him.' Now I have told you."

—MATTHEW 28:2–7

"The resurrection is the keystone of the arch on which our faith is supported. If Christ has not risen, we must impeach all those witnesses for lying. If Christ has not risen, we have no proof that the crucifixion of Jesus differed from that of the two thieves who suffered with him. If Christ has not risen, it is impossible to believe his atoning death was accepted."

—D. L. MOODY

"Our Lord has written the promise of resurrection,
not in books alone but in every leaf in springtime."
—Martin Luther

No matter what a believer in Christ may or may not accomplish
in the course of a lifetime, that individual can rely on this unchange-
able truth: "I will one day stand in the very presence of God's Son,
my Creator and Savior."

He was handed over to die because of our sins, and
he was raised to life to make us right with God.
—Romans 4:25 NLT

"According to the laws of legal evidence used in courts of law, there is more evidence for the historical fact of the resurrection of Jesus Christ than for just about any other event in history."

—SIMON GREENLEAF

"Well, then, look at the facts in this case. The Saviour is working mightily among men, every day He is invisibly persuading numbers of people all over the world, both within and beyond the Greek-speaking world, to accept His faith and be obedient to His teaching. Can anyone, in face of this, still doubt that He has risen and lives, or rather that He is Himself the Life? Does a dead man prick the consciences of men . . . ?"

—ATHANASIUS

When the disciples understood at last that Jesus had unlocked the door of the final enemy, death itself, they no longer hid from lesser enemies behind locked doors.

All honor to God, the God and Father of our Lord Jesus Christ; for it is his boundless mercy that has given us the privilege of being born again so that we are now members of God's own family. Now we live in the hope of eternal life because Christ rose again from the dead.

—1 PETER 1:3 TLB

"After he had once ascended to the Father, he not only appeared to his disciples again and again, but their hands handled the word of life, and he ate in their presence. He had been to his Father, and had returned that they might know him lifted above the grave and all that region in which death has power; that as the elder brother, free of the oppressions of humanity, but fulfilled of its tenderness, he might show himself captain of their salvation."

—GEORGE MACDONALD

"We shall with these eyes behold our Lord when he shall stand in the latter day upon the earth. O glorious resurrection, which has turned our poison into medicine! O miracle of love, which has made death to be the gate of life!"

—CHARLES SPURGEON

Jesus our Shepherd and Leader has gone on ahead of us, entering death and the grave and ascending to heaven to prepare for our arrival.

"The way to the tomb may be hard, as it was for Him; but we who look on, see the hardness and not the help; we see the suffering but not the sustaining: that is known only to the dying and God. They can tell us little of this, and nothing of the glad safety beyond."

—GEORGE MACDONALD

"A dead Christ I must do everything for;
a living Christ does everything for me."

—ANDREW MURRAY

Now if we died with Christ, we believe that we will
also live with him. For we know that since Christ
was raised from the dead, he cannot die again;
death no longer has mastery over him.

—ROMANS 6:8–9

"But as for me, I know that my Redeemer lives,
and that he will stand upon the earth at last. And
I know that after this body has decayed, this body
shall see God! Then he will be on my side! Yes, I
shall see him, not as a stranger, but as a friend!
What a glorious hope!"

—JOB 19:25–27 TLB

"I was all the time tugging and carrying water. But
now I have a river that carries me."

—D. L. MOODY

"I believe in
the Holy Spirit. . . ."

*I*f we truly understood even for a moment what sort of Companion, Counselor, and Friend we have in the Holy Spirit, it would banish all thoughts of loneliness forever.

> "If you love me, obey me; and I will ask the Father and he will give you another Comforter, and he will never leave you. He is the Holy Spirit, the Spirit who leads into all truth. The world at large cannot receive him, for it isn't looking for him and doesn't recognize him. But you do, for he lives with you now and someday shall be in you."
>
> —JOHN 14:15–17 TLB

> "You might as well try to see without eyes, hear without ears, or breathe without lungs, as to try to live the Christian life without the Holy Spirit."
>
> —D. L. MOODY

"I seek the will of the Spirit of God through or in connection with the Word of God. The Spirit and the Word must be combined. If I look to the Spirit alone without the Word, I lay myself open to great delusions also."

—George Mueller

Hope through the Holy Spirit isn't like a well where we let down a bucket; it is a river that will carry us through anything.

May the God of hope fill you with all joy and peace as you trust in him, so that you may overflow with hope by the power of the Holy Spirit.

—Romans 15:13

"O Holy Spirit, descend plentifully into my heart. Enlighten the dark corners of this neglected dwelling and scatter there Thy cheerful beams."

—Augustine

"Men ought to seek with their whole hearts to be filled with the Spirit of God. Without being filled with the Spirit, it is utterly impossible that an individual Christian or a church can ever live or work as God desires."

—Andrew Murray

And because we are his children, God has sent the Spirit of his Son into our hearts, prompting us to call out, "Abba, Father."

—Galatians 4:6 nlt

Weakness and frailty are no hindrances to God's Spirit. He isn't looking for human strength, He is looking for submissive hearts—men and women who allow Him to release His strength through them.

> The Holy Spirit helps us in our weakness. For example, we don't know what God wants us to pray for. But the Holy Spirit prays for us with groanings that cannot be expressed in words. And the Father who knows all hearts knows what the Spirit is saying, for the Spirit pleads for us believers in harmony with God's own will.
>
> —ROMANS 8:26–27 NLT

> "It was the Lord who put into my mind that fact that it would be possible to sail from here to the Indies. All who heard of my project rejected it with laughter, ridiculing me. There is no question that the inspiration was from the Holy Spirit, because He comforted me with rays of marvelous inspiration from the Holy Scriptures."
>
> —CHRISTOPHER COLUMBUS

> "But when they arrest you, do not worry about what to say or how to say it. At that time you will be given what to say, for it will not be you speaking, but the Spirit of your Father speaking through you."
>
> —MATTHEW 10:19–20

> "The presence of the Holy Spirit is the keystone of all our hopes."
>
> —JOHN NELSON DARBY

The Holy Spirit fills a man or woman's spirit the way a fresh breeze fills a sail. This speaks of power, direction, and progress toward new horizons.

"Without the Spirit of God, we can do nothing. We are as ships without wind. We are useless."

—Charles Spurgeon

"Our heart oft times wakes when we sleep, and God can speak to that, either by words, by proverbs, by signs and similitudes, as well as if one was awake."

—John Bunyan

"Whenever we see the Word of God purely preached and heard, there a church of God exists, even if it swarms with many faults."

—John Calvin

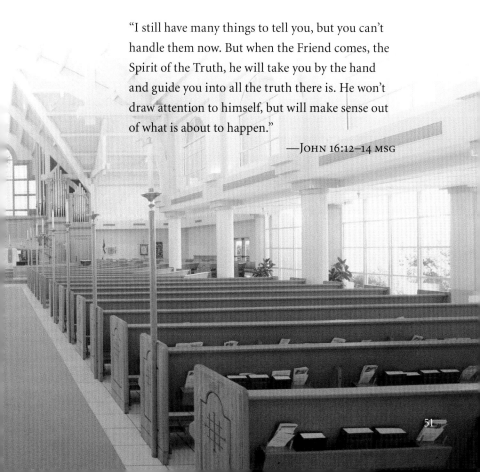

"What the Church needs today is not more machinery or better, not new organizations or more and novel methods, but men whom the Holy Spirit can use—men of prayer, men mighty in prayer. The Holy Spirit does not flow through methods, but through men. He does not come on machinery, but on men. He does not anoint plans, but men, men of prayer."

—E. M. Bounds

"I still have many things to tell you, but you can't handle them now. But when the Friend comes, the Spirit of the Truth, he will take you by the hand and guide you into all the truth there is. He won't draw attention to himself, but will make sense out of what is about to happen."

—John 16:12–14 MSG

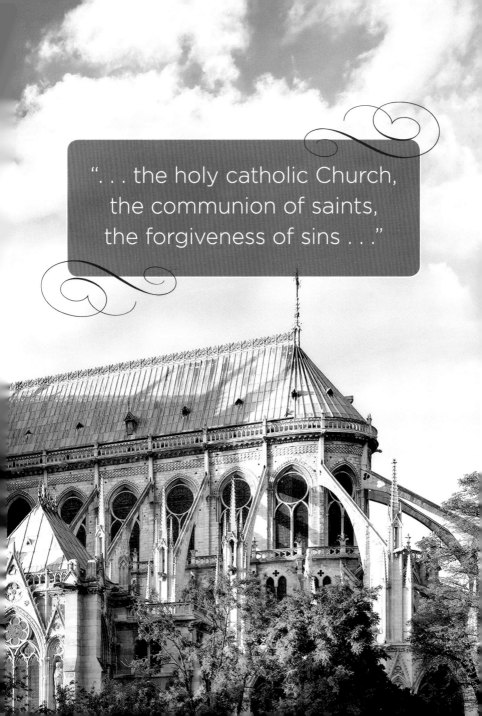

". . . the holy catholic Church,
the communion of saints,
the forgiveness of sins . . ."

Roberto Sydney
Beati qui habitant

Aloysio Hay, obiit 25
in domo Domini

Iul. MDCCCLXXXV.
Psalm. LXXXIII. 5.

*S*cattered across the globe, from one corner of our world to the other, in the most inhospitable, out-of-the-way, unlikely places imaginable, the Lord has His people.

> *"Christ has no body now but yours*
> *No hands, no feet on earth but yours*
> *Yours are the eyes through which he looks*
> *compassion on this world*
> *Yours are the feet with which*
> *He walks to do good*
> *Yours are the hands with which*
> *He blesses all the world."*
>
> —Theresa of Avila

> Jesus . . . said, "Who do you think my mother and brothers are?" He then stretched out his hand toward his disciples. "Look closely. These are my mother and brothers."
>
> —Matthew 12:48–49 msg

> "Faith simply means: What I am seeking is not here, and for that very reason I believe it. Faith expressly signifies the deep, strong, blessed restlessness that drives the believer so that he cannot settle down at rest in this world."
>
> —Søren Kierkegaard

Christians who convince themselves they can "go it alone," pushing through life without the encouragement, wisdom, accountability, and care of brothers and sisters in Christ, have deeply impoverished themselves.

"The church is no more religion than the masonry of the aqueduct is the water that flows through it."

—Henry Ward Beecher

"Church attendance is as vital to a disciple as a transfusion of rich, healthy blood to a sick man."

—D. L. Moody

God has put all things under the authority of Christ and has made him head over all things for the benefit of the church. And the church is his body; it is made full and complete by Christ, who fills all things everywhere with himself.

—Ephesians 1:22–23 nlt

Jesus replied, "Blessed are you, Simon son of Jonah, for this was not revealed to you by flesh and blood, but by my Father in heaven. And I tell you that you are Peter, and on this rock I will build my church, and the gates of Hades will not overcome it."

—Matthew 16:17–18

God has given each of us gifts that we will never discover until we willingly step into the life of a fellow believer to offer our help.

> Since you are so anxious to have special gifts from the Holy Spirit, ask him for the very best, for those that will be of real help to the whole church.
>
> —1 CORINTHIANS 14:12 TLB

> "Going to church doesn't make you a Christian any more than going to a garage makes you an automobile."
>
> —BILLY SUNDAY

> For the Lord himself will come down from heaven, with a loud command, with the voice of the archangel and with the trumpet call of God, and the dead in Christ will rise first. After that, we who are still alive and are left will be caught up together with them in the clouds to meet the Lord in the air. And so we will be with the Lord forever. Therefore encourage one another with these words.
>
> —1 THESSALONIANS 4:16–18

> "Nothing doth so much keep men out of the Church, and drive men out of the Church, as breach of unity."
>
> —FRANCIS BACON

Those who have walked in the faith centuries before us and those who may follow after us centuries from now will one day be as familiar and dear to us as the faces we see every day. In heaven, the separation of years will melt away forever.

"An humble spire, pointing heavenward from an obscure church, speaks of man's nature, man's dignity, man's destiny, more eloquently than all the columns and arches of Greece and Rome, the mausoleums of Asia, or the pyramids of Egypt."

—WILLIAM E. CHANNING

Don't just pretend to love others. Really love them. Hate what is wrong. Hold tightly to what is good. Love each other with genuine affection, and take delight in honoring each other. Never be lazy, but work hard and serve the Lord enthusiastically. Rejoice in our confident hope. Be patient in trouble, and keep on praying. When God's people are in need, be ready to help them. Always be eager to practice hospitality.

—ROMANS 12:9–13 NLT

"The day we find the perfect church, it becomes imperfect the moment we join it."

—CHARLES SPURGEON

"The blood of the martyrs is the seed of the church."

—TERTULLIAN

"Eternity is the divine treasure-house, and hope is the window, by means of which mortals are permitted to see, as through a glass darkly, the things which God is preparing."

—WILLIAM MOUNTFORD

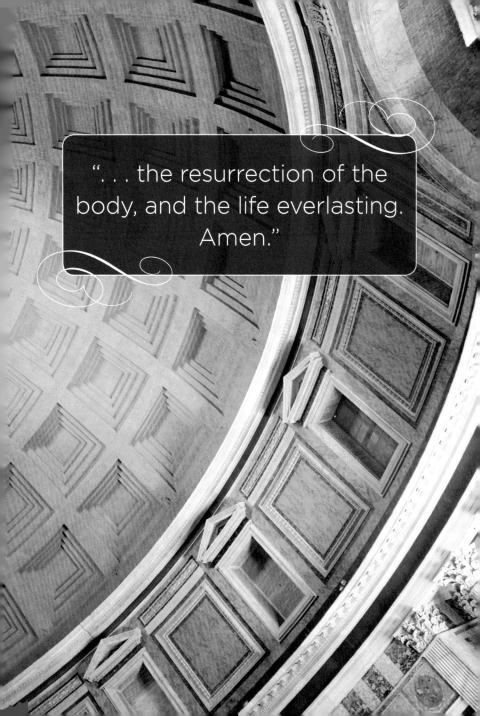

"... the resurrection of the body, and the life everlasting. Amen."

$\mathcal{I}$t isn't death that claims our loved ones in Christ; it is everlasting life. In the final moments, life presses in, and ultimately swallows our fragile human existence in a wave of light, release, and inexpressible joy.

> "My beliefs teach me to feel as safe in battle as in bed.
> God has fixed the time of my death. I do not concern
> myself with that, but to be always ready whenever it
> may overtake me. That is the way all men should live,
> and all men should be equally brave."
>
> —STONEWALL JACKSON

"Among the many signs of a lively faith and hope
we have in eternal life, one of the surest signs is not
being overly sad at the death of those whom we dearly
love in our Lord."

—IGNATIUS

Multitudes who sleep in the dust of the earth will
awake: some to everlasting life, others to shame and
everlasting contempt. Those who are wise will shine like
the brightness of the heavens, and those who lead many
to righteousness, like the stars for ever and ever.

—DANIEL 12:2–3

We may dread the shadow of death, but it is only a shadow. In
our last moments, we pass through the shadow into eternal morning.

"Eternity to the godly is a day that has no sunset;
eternity to the wicked is a night that has no sunrise."

—THOMAS WATSON

Jesus replied, "Marriage is for people here on earth.
But in the age to come, those worthy of being raised
from the dead will neither marry nor be given in
marriage. And they will never die again. In this
respect they will be like angels. They are children of
God and children of the resurrection."

—LUKE 20:34–36 NLT

"As winter strips the leaves from around us, so
that we may see the distant regions they formerly
concealed, so old age takes away our enjoyments only
to enlarge the prospects of the coming eternity."

—JEAN PAUL RICHTER

Death was never part of God's plan for humankind. In the end, the very memory of it will fade as a bad dream fades in a bright room over coffee and breakfast with laughing friends.

> For if we have been united with him in a death like his, we shall certainly be united with him in a resurrection like his.
>
> —ROMANS 6:5 ESV

> But Christ has indeed been raised from the dead, the firstfruits of those who have fallen asleep. For since death came through a man, the resurrection of the dead comes also through a man. For as in Adam all die, so in Christ all will be made alive.
>
> —1 CORINTHIANS 15:20–22

> "Yes, from the mountain of eternity we shall look down, and behold the whole plain spread before us. Down here we get lost and confused in the devious valleys that run off from the roots of the hills everywhere, and we cannot make out where the streams are going, and what is beyond that low shoulder of the hill yonder. But when we get to the summit and look down, it will all shape itself into one consistent whole, and we shall see it all at once."
>
> —THOMAS BOSTON

We live out our lives on earth in temporary shelters—tents that tear, sag, leak, or unravel after years of use. The new body we step into when we leave the old one behind will outlast the stars.

"The world which stretches out before you is but the vestibule of immortal life. These deeds that are taking place around you touch upon chords that extend by a thousand connections, visible and invisible, and vibrate in eternity."

—Edwin Hubbell Chapin

"Very truly I tell you, whoever hears my word and believes him who sent me has eternal life and will not be judged but has crossed over from death to life."

—John 5:24

"Someday you will read in the papers that Moody is dead. Don't you believe a word of it. At that moment I shall be more alive than I am now. I was born of the flesh in 1837, I was born of the spirit in 1855. That which is born of the flesh may die. That which is born of the Spirit shall live forever."

—D. L. Moody

"And this is the will of God, that I should not lose even one of all those he has given me, but that I should raise them to eternal life at the Last Day. For it is my Father's will that everyone who sees his Son and believes on him should have eternal life— that I should raise him at the Last Day."

—John 6:39–40 TLB

The Nicene Creed

We believe in one God, the Father, the Almighty maker of heaven and earth, of all that is, seen and unseen.

We believe in one Lord, Jesus Christ, the only Son of God, eternally begotten of the Father,

God from God, Light from Light, true God from true God, begotten, not made, of one Being with the Father.

Through Him all things were made.

For us men and for our salvation He came down from heaven: by the power of the Holy Spirit He became incarnate from the Virgin Mary, and was made man.

For our sake He was crucified under Pontius Pilate; He suffered death and was buried.

On the third day He rose again in accordance with the Scriptures; He ascended into heaven and is seated at the right hand of the Father.

He will come again in glory to judge the living and the dead, and His kingdom will have no end.

We believe in the Holy Spirit, the Lord, the giver of Life, who proceeds from the Father and the Son. With the Father and the Son He is worshipped and glorified.

He has spoken through the Prophets.

We believe in one holy catholic and apostolic Church.

We acknowledge one baptism for the forgiveness of sins.

We look for the resurrection of the dead, and the life of the world to come.

Amen.

"The vision of God is indeed the transfiguration of the world."

—Brooke Foss Westcott

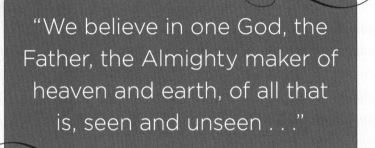

"We believe in one God, the Father, the Almighty maker of heaven and earth, of all that is, seen and unseen . . ."

*T*o believe in the Creator is to look for His signature in nature, whether exceedingly large or minute beyond the limits of our vision. We see His initials in the great constellations wheeling across a summer sky, in the smile of a little child, and on the wings of a bee, immersed in a daisy.

> All things were created through him and for him.
>
> —Colossians 1:16 esv

> "'Who gathered this flower?' The gardener answered, 'The Master.' And his fellow servant held his peace."
>
> —Unknown

> "Be glad; rejoice forever in my creation!"
>
> —Isaiah 65:18 nlt

"Understanding is the reward of faith. Therefore seek not to understand that you may believe, but believe that you may understand."

—AUGUSTINE

"As the sun does its work in the weak one who seeks its rays, God will do His work in you."

—ANDREW MURRAY

We have not visited with angels or seen where they live. We have not peered into the eternal realm or strolled tree-lined avenues of transparent gold. But we have seen snowflakes dancing in the wind, great storm clouds gathering on the horizon, and a butterfly resting with folded wings. We can easily believe in God's invisible creation, because of what we have witnessed in the visible.

"What good is an idol carved by man, or a cast image that deceives you? How foolish to trust in your own creation—a god that can't even talk!"

—HABAKKUK 2:18 NLT

"Thou must begin low, and be glad of a little light to travel with, and be faithful thereunto; and in faithfulness expect additions of light, and so much power as may help thee to rub on. And though you may be long weak and little and ready to perish; yet the Father will help thee, and cause His life to shoot up in thee."

—ISAAC PENINGTON

The created world itself can hardly wait for what's coming next. Everything in creation is being more or less held back. God reins it in until both creation and all the creatures are ready and can be released at the same moment into the glorious times ahead. Meanwhile, the joyful anticipation deepens.

—ROMANS 8:18–21 MSG

A loving father speaks courage into the hearts of his sons and daughters, takes pleasure in their every accomplishment, and stands by to help in times of danger, sorrow, or weakness. So it is with our Father in heaven, the one from whom all good fathers derive their name.

"We know what God is like
because we know the character of Jesus Christ."
—GEORGE HODGES

May you always be filled with the fruit of your salvation—the righteous character produced in your life by Jesus Christ—for this will bring much glory and praise to God.

—PHILIPPIANS 1:11 NLT

The Son radiates God's own glory and expresses the very character of God, and he sustains everything by the mighty power of his command. When he had cleansed us from our sins, he sat down in the place of honor at the right hand of the majestic God in heaven.

—HEBREWS 1:3 NLT

The only thing an Almighty God cannot do is to act against His own character and nature.

"Am I not present everywhere, whether seen or unseen?"

—Jeremiah 23:24 MSG

"Beware in your prayers, above everything else, of limiting God, not only by unbelief, but by fancying that you know what He can do."

—Andrew Murray

We look not to the things that are seen but to the things that are unseen. For the things that are seen are transient, but the things that are unseen are eternal.

—2 Corinthians 4:18 ESV

"Seek not to understand that you may believe, but believe that you may understand."

—Augustine

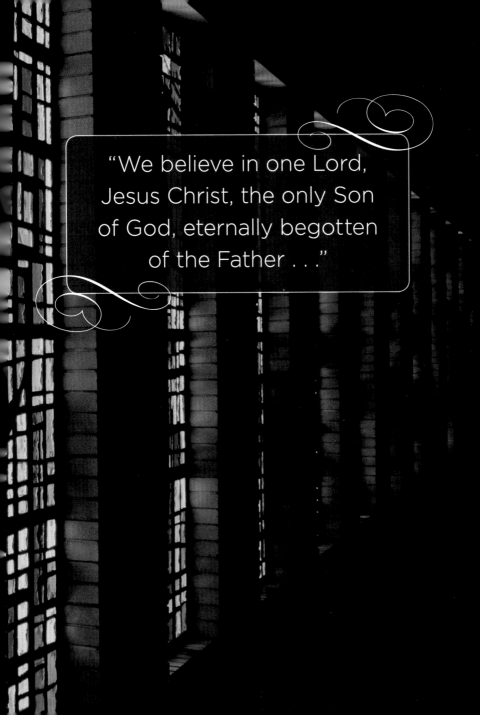

"We believe in one Lord, Jesus Christ, the only Son of God, eternally begotten of the Father . . ."

While life may seem complicated at times, it really all comes down to this: Jesus, the perfect Son of God, died for our sins on a Roman cross, was raised from the dead, and offers Himself today as our Lord, Savior, and constant Friend. This is the essence of life, both here and in the world to come.

> Could it be any clearer? Our old way of life was nailed to the cross with Christ, a decisive end to that sin-miserable life—no longer at sin's every beck and call! What we believe is this: If we get included in Christ's sin-conquering death, we also get included in his life-saving resurrection. We know that when Jesus was raised from the dead it was a signal of the end of death-as-the-end. Never again will death have the last word. When Jesus died, he took sin down with him, but alive he brings God down to us. From now on, think of it this way: Sin speaks a dead language that means nothing to you; God speaks your mother tongue, and you hang on every word. You are dead to sin and alive to God. That's what Jesus did.
>
> —Romans 6:6–11 msg

> "Never try to arouse faith from within. You cannot stir up faith from the depths of your heart. Leave your heart, and look into the face of Christ."
>
> —Andrew Murray

> *The meaning of Jesus Christ's death was made as clear to you as if you had seen a picture of his death on the cross.*
>
> —Galatians 3:1 nlt

Christ reconciled both groups to God by means
of his death on the cross, and our hostility toward
each other was put to death.

—Ephesians 2:16 nlt

Hope isn't a wish, a preference, a desire, or a longing; hope is a Person, the Lord Jesus Christ. Without Him, human plans and dreams are little more than shimmering mirages in the desert. With Him and in Him, hope has no boundaries at all.

"For the Lord touched all parts of creation, and
freed and undeceived them all from every deceit."

—Athanasius

"Is not your fear of God your confidence,
and the integrity of your ways your hope?"

—Job 4:6 esv

"GOD brings death and GOD brings life,
brings down to the grave and raises up.
GOD brings poverty and GOD brings wealth;
he lowers, he also lifts up.
He puts poor people on their feet again;
he rekindles burned-out lives with fresh hope,
Restoring dignity and respect to their lives—
a place in the sun!"

—1 SAMUEL 2:6–7 MSG

The name of Jesus both attracts and repels. To those who seek Him or already love Him, His name carries an unmistakable fragrance of life. To those who try to shut Him out, deny Him, or ignore Him, His name offends, annoys, or even angers. No one is truly indifferent to the name of Jesus.

"If, retiring into solitude for a portion of each day, we should select some one scene or trait or incident in the life of Jesus, and with all the helps we can get seek to understand it fully, tracing it in the other evangelists, comparing it with other passages of Scripture, etc., we should find ourselves insensibly interested, and might hope that, in this effort of our souls to understand Him, Jesus Himself would draw near, as He did of old to the disciples on the way to Emmaus."

—HARRIET BEECHER STOWE

At the name of Jesus every knee should bow,
in heaven and on earth and under the earth.

—PHILIPPIANS 2:10 NLT

80

"Christ by His coming has made our abiding inheritance."

—BROOKE FOSS WESTCOTT

What could an infinite, eternal, invisible, all-knowing, all-powerful Being do to make Himself approachable to men, women, and small children? He could be born to a poor teenage Jewish girl in a tiny, occupied nation, learn the trade of a carpenter, teach the very words of God, heal bodies and hearts, and finally offer Himself for the sins of the world.

"Amor vincit omnia (love conquers all)."

—CHAUCER, *Canterbury Tales*

"The life I live it is not mine,
Thy will, my will, have made it Thine."

—ELIZABETH PRENTISS

"A rule I have had for years is: to treat the Lord Jesus Christ as a personal friend. His is not a creed, a mere doctrine, but it is He Himself we have."

—D. L. MOODY

"All God's giants have been weak men who did great things for God because they reckoned on God being with them."

—HUDSON TAYLOR

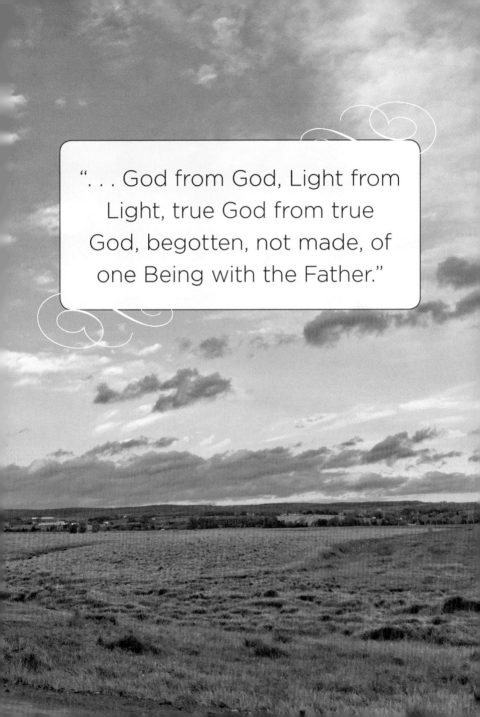

". . . God from God, Light from Light, true God from true God, begotten, not made, of one Being with the Father."

From eternity past, the God-in-Three-Persons, Father, Son, and Holy Spirit, enjoyed perfect, complete, joyful unity and companionship. Then, for reasons beyond our grasp, God chose to grant the miracle of human life. Through Christ, He offers a gift vastly greater than this—an eternity with Himself. This second gift of life, however, must be received by a deliberate choice.

> *"Death may be the King of terrors . . .*
> *but Jesus is the King of kings!"*
>
> —D. L. Moody

> The peace of God, which transcends all under-
> standing, will guard your hearts and your minds in
> Christ Jesus.
>
> —Philippians 4:7

*"O, let the place of secret prayer become to me
the most beloved spot on earth."*

—ANDREW MURRAY

God is the creator and source of light. All light that ever was or will be begins in Him. When the darkness of sorrow, confusion, anxiety, or loneliness descends, He invites us into a light-filled refuge where we can rest and heal.

"Humility is perfect quietness of heart. It is to expect nothing, to wonder at nothing that is done to me, to feel nothing done against me. It is to be at rest when nobody praises me, and when I am blamed or despised. It is to have a blessed home in the Lord, where I can go in and shut the door, and kneel to my Father in secret, and am at peace as in a deep sea of calmness, when all around and above is trouble."

—ANDREW MURRAY

"Humility like darkness reveals the heavenly lights."

—HENRY DAVID THOREAU

"Are you tired? Worn out? Burned out on religion? Come to me. Get away with me and you'll recover your life. I'll show you how to take a real rest. Walk with me and work with me—watch how I do it. Learn the unforced rhythms of grace. I won't lay anything heavy or ill-fitting on you. Keep company with me and you'll learn to live freely and lightly."

—MATTHEW 11:28–30 MSG

*"Just as water ever seeks and fills the lowest place, so the
moment God finds you abased and empty,
His glory and power flow in."*

—ANDREW MURRAY

Jesus said to His friend, "Don't you know me, Philip? . . . Anyone who has seen me has seen the Father" (John 14:9). The infinite, invisible God became a seeable, touchable human being, who spoke with a young man's voice and touched the hurting and hopeless with the warm, calloused hands of a Jewish carpenter. He went to unimaginable lengths to reveal Himself to us. He wants to be known.

*"Would you be free from the burden of sin?
There's pow'r in the blood, pow'r in the blood;
Would you o'er evil a victory win?
There's wonderful pow'r in the blood."*

—LEWIS E. JONES

"You don't have to wait for the End. I am, right
now, Resurrection and Life. The one who believes
in me, even though he or she dies, will live. And
everyone who lives believing in me does not ultimately die at all. Do you believe this?"

—JOHN 11:25–26 MSG

*"God created the world out of nothing,
and so long as we are nothing,
He can make something out of us."*

—MARTIN LUTHER

None of us feels whole in ourselves. We have unfulfilled dreams, frustrated ambitions, desires that fall short, and empty places in our souls. Yet for all of that, we are complete in Jesus Christ. The more we walk with Him, the more we will see it.

"Humility is the proper estimate of oneself."

—Charles Spurgeon

"The sufficiency of my merit is to know that my merit is not sufficient."

—Augustine

Pride leads to disgrace, but with humility comes wisdom.

—Proverbs 11:2 NLT

"Christ is the humility of God embodied in human nature; the Eternal Love humbling itself, clothing itself in the garb of meekness and gentleness, to win and serve and save us."

—Andrew Murray

". . .That which has been believed everywhere, always, and by all."

—Vincent of Lerins

"Through Him all things were made."

*W*hen we find ourselves moved by the beauty of a spring morning or the soaring majesty of a snow-capped mountain or a calm ocean at sunset, we have the privilege of actually telling the Maker and Creator of these things how we feel. In fact, that is what He intended from the beginning.

> "You search the Scriptures because you think they give you eternal life. But the Scriptures point to me!"
> —John 5:39 nlt

> "Men ought to seek with their whole hearts to be filled with the Spirit of God. Without being filled with the Spirit, it is utterly impossible that an individual Christian or a church can ever live or work as God desires."
> —Andrew Murray

> "Be assured, if you walk with Him and look to Him, and expect help from Him, He will never fail you."
> —George Mueller

True followers of Jesus are happy people because they know a truth that allows the whole jigsaw puzzle of life on earth to make sense: An intelligent, loving design underlies everything in the earth and heavens—including our very lives.

> Give me happiness, O Lord, for I give myself to you.
> —Psalm 86:4 nlt

"When large numbers of people share their joy in common, the happiness of each is greater because each adds fuel to the other's flame."

—AUGUSTINE

"It is not how much we have, but how much we enjoy, that makes happiness."

—CHARLES SPURGEON

The One who made and sustains all things most certainly understands all things . . . including the life situations which from our perspective seem "too complicated" or "too late" or "too involved." When we can't see or even imagine a way out, He can.

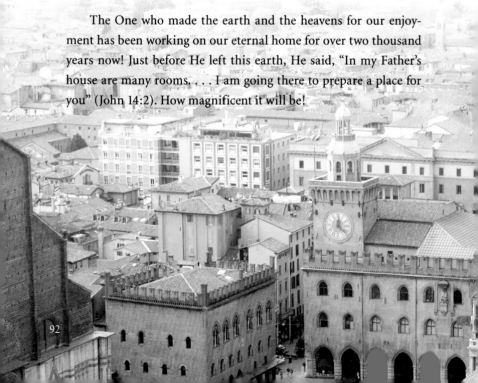

"God has no pleasure in afflicting us, but He will not keep back even the most painful chastisement if He can but thereby guide His beloved child to come home and abide in the beloved Son."

—Andrew Murray

"I am not what I ought to be. I am not what I want to be. I am not what I hope to be. But still, I am not what I used to be. And by the grace of God, I am what I am."

—John Newton

Those who live in the shelter of the Most High
will find rest in the shadow of the Almighty.

—Psalm 91:1 nlt

The One who made the earth and the heavens for our enjoyment has been working on our eternal home for over two thousand years now! Just before He left this earth, He said, "In my Father's house are many rooms, . . . I am going there to prepare a place for you" (John 14:2). How magnificent it will be!

"Enter through the narrow gate. For wide is the gate and broad is the road that leads to destruction, and many enter through it. But small is the gate and narrow the road that leads to life, and only a few find it."

—Matthew 7:13–14

"One should go to sleep as homesick passengers do, saying, 'Perhaps in the morning we shall see the shore.'"

—Henry Ward Beecher

"The body of the Word, then, being a real human body, in spite of its having been uniquely formed from a virgin, was of itself mortal and, like other bodies, liable to death. But the indwelling of the Word loosed it from this natural liability, so that corruption could not touch it."

—Athanasius

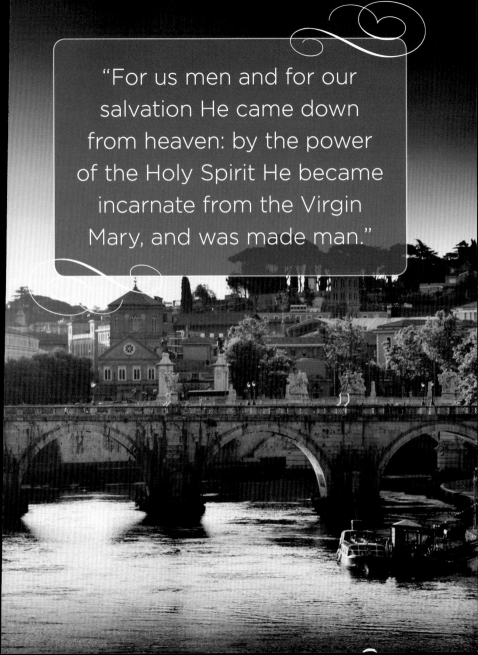

"For us men and for our salvation He came down from heaven: by the power of the Holy Spirit He became incarnate from the Virgin Mary, and was made man."

*I*t is one thing to be rescued from death and destruction. It is another thing to be rescued by One who came before we were born, gave Himself for sins we had not yet committed, and purchased our entrance to the next life before we lived one moment in this one.

> Jesus gave his life for our sins, just as God our Father planned, in order to rescue us from this evil world in which we live.
> —GALATIANS 1:4 NLT

> For he has rescued us from the kingdom of darkness and transferred us into the Kingdom of his dear Son.
> —COLOSSIANS 1:13 NLT

> "The Self-revealing of the Word is in every dimension—above, in creation; below, in the Incarnation; in the depth, in Hades; in the breadth, throughout the world. All things have been filled with the knowledge of God."
> —ATHANASIUS

Jesus already knew every sin we would ever commit and paid the full price and penalty for those offenses against God before we ever came to be. There is no sin that He didn't pay for. We can walk in complete forgiveness with our Creator and Savior.

> *I am writing to you who are God's children*
> *because your sins have been forgiven through Jesus.*
> —1 JOHN 2:12 NLT

"This message [should] be proclaimed in the authority of his name to all the nations, beginning in Jerusalem: 'There is forgiveness of sins for all who repent.'"

—LUKE 24:47 NLT

"He that cannot forgive others, breaks the bridge over which he himself must pass if he would ever reach heaven; for everyone has need to be forgiven."

—GEORGE HERBERT

Jesus became a man—a real human being—so that He might experience life in the very same way that we do, apart from our sins. No one can ever say to Jesus, "You don't understand. You don't know what it's like . . ."

"The Lord did not come to make a display. He came to heal and to teach suffering men. For one who wanted to make a display the thing would have been just to appear and dazzle the beholders. But for Him Who came to heal and to teach the way was not merely to dwell here, but to put Himself at the disposal of those who needed Him, and to be manifested according as they could bear it, not vitiating the value of the Divine appearing by exceeding their capacity to receive it."

—ATHANASIUS

"For the Lord touched all parts of creation, and freed and undeceived them all from every deceit."

—ATHANASIUS

So the Word became human and made his home
among us. He was full of unfailing love and faithfulness. And we have seen his glory, the glory of the
Father's one and only Son.

—JOHN 1:14 NLT

Jesus was born of a godly young teenage girl. Part of His experience
of humanity included the warm security of the womb, the trauma of
being born, and the sudden change in entering a world filled with new
sights, smells, sounds, and sensations. For Jesus, it was on a starlit night
with the smell of wood, hay, and animals . . . and perhaps the echo of
angel voices from the nearby fields.

"God had one son on earth without sin,
but never one without suffering."

—AUGUSTINE

"The Lord himself will give you the sign. Look! The virgin will conceive a child! She will give birth to a son and
will call him Immanuel (which means 'God is with us')."

—ISAIAH 7:14 NLT

"Our God, Jesus Christ, was, according to the
appointment of God, conceived in the womb by
Mary, of the seed of David, but by the Holy Spirit."

—IGNATIUS

"Yet, because the Word was in it, death and corruption were in the same act utterly abolished."

—ATHANASIUS

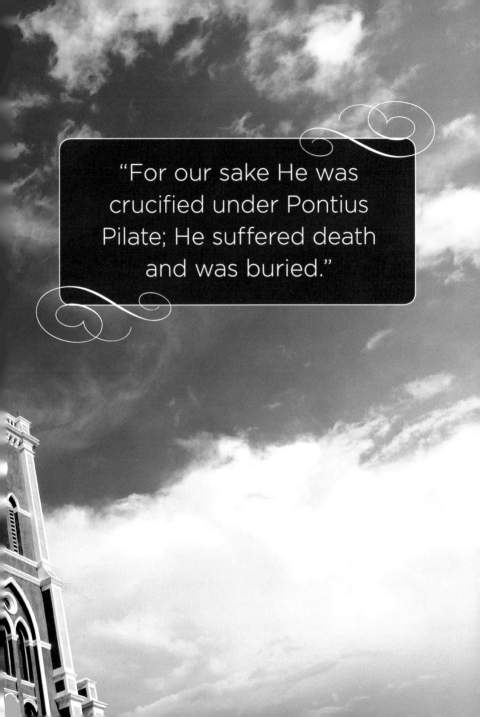

"For our sake He was crucified under Pontius Pilate; He suffered death and was buried."

*J*esus was a strong young man who lived life to the full, and He didn't want to die. Everything in His humanity wanted to cling to life, and shrank from the torture, suffering, and shameful death that loomed ahead of Him. But He kept to the dark path and finally gave Himself over to the will of evil men . . . because He knew the eternal difference it would make to each one of us.

> "O, let us understand that the power of Christianity lies not in a hazy indefiniteness, not in shadowy forms, not so much even in definite truths and doctrines, but in the truth and the doctrine. There is but one Christ crucified. All the gathered might of the infinite God is in that word."
> —HERRICK JOHNSON

> "God's beloved Son, leaving the echoes of His cries upon the mountains and the traces of His weary feet upon the streets, shedding His tears over the tombs and His blood upon Golgotha, associating His life with our homes, and His corpse with our sepulchres, shows us how we, too, may be sons in the humblest vale of life, and sure of sympathy in heaven amid the deepest wrongs and sorrows of earth."
> —EDWARD THOMSON

> But God knew what would happen, and his prearranged plan was carried out when Jesus was betrayed. With the help of lawless Gentiles, you nailed him to a cross and killed him.
> —ACTS 2:23 NLT

The Author of life willingly embraced death, so that none who live would have to fear death again. For those who belong to Christ, death is nothing more than a shadowy doorway into endless life with Him.

> And regarding the question, friends, that has come
> up about what happens to those already dead and
> buried, we don't want you in the dark any longer.
> First off, you must not carry on over them like
> people who have nothing to look forward to, as if
> the grave were the last word. Since Jesus died and
> broke loose from the grave, God will most certainly
> bring back to life those who died in Jesus.
>
> —1 Thessalonians 4:13–14 msg

"[God] wants you to have something far better than riches and gold, and that is helpless dependence upon Him."

—Hudson Taylor

"It is not darkness you are going to, for God is Light. It is not lonely, for Christ is with you. It is not unknown country, for Christ is there."

—Charles Kingsley

"O to grace how great a debtor
Daily I'm constrained to be!
Let Thy goodness, like a fetter,
Bind my wandering heart to Thee.
Prone to wander, Lord, I feel it,
Prone to leave the God I love;
Here's my heart, O take and seal it,
Seal it for Thy courts above."

—Robert Robinson

Pontius Pilate stood within mere inches of the One whose very name is Truth, and muttered, "What is truth?" For those who desire it, the real truth about life and life-beyond-life is as near as an open Bible and a heart cry to Jesus.

"When the time comes for you to die, you need not be afraid, because death cannot separate you from God's love."

—Charles Spurgeon

Jesus said to her, "I am the resurrection and the life. The one who believes in me will live, even though they die; and whoever lives by believing in me will never die. Do you believe this?"

—John 11:25–26

"Christian! Death cannot hurt you! Death is your best friend—who is commissioned by Christ to summon you from the world of vanity and woe, and from a body of sin and death—to the blissful regions of glory and immortality, to meet your Lord, and to be forever with Him!"

—William Mason

When the dead body of Jesus was placed in a sealed tomb, the authorities had every reason to expect that was where He would stay. But Jesus has a way of breaking through every barrier designed by men or hell. No earthly authority or expectation—or even death itself—can keep Him from rescuing men and women who call out to Him in faith.

"All other great men are valued for their lives; He, above all, for His death, around which mercy and truth, righteousness and peace, God and man are reconciled."

—Edward Thomson

"Lord Jesus, you embraced your cross to redeem the world. Help me to embrace the crosses in my life—the hardships, struggles, disappointments, pain. Only by recognizing my own weakness, can I discover your strength."

—Unknown

For the message of the cross is foolishness to those who are perishing, but to us who are being saved it is the power of God.

—1 Corinthians 1:18

"On the third day He rose again in accordance with the Scriptures; He ascended into heaven and is seated at the right hand of the Father."

*D*avid wrote, "Weeping may stay for the night, but rejoicing comes in the morning" (Psalm 30:5). Those words came to their ultimate fulfillment when Jesus, the Son of David, defeated death and walked into a Sunday morning sunrise.

> *". . . My sin, not in part but the whole,*
> *Is nailed to His cross, and I bear it no more,*
> *Praise the Lord, praise the Lord, O my soul!*
> *And Lord haste the day, when my faith shall be sight,*
> *The clouds be rolled back as a scroll;*
> *The trump shall resound, and the Lord shall descend,*
> *Even so, it is well with my soul."*
>
> —HORATIO SPAFFORD

> *"God had an only Son,*
> *and He was a missionary and a physician."*
>
> —DAVID LIVINGSTONE

Who then will condemn us? No one—for Christ
Jesus died for us and was raised to life for us, and
he is sitting in the place of honor at God's right
hand, pleading for us.

—ROMANS 8:34 NLT

All of the darkest, saddest, most terrible nights our world has
ever known are counterbalanced by one early morning in Israel
when holy angels rolled the stone away from an empty tomb and
proclaimed, "He is risen!"

"Christ is not valued at all unless he be valued
above all."

—AUGUSTINE

Have this attitude in yourselves which was also in
Christ Jesus, who, although He existed in the form
of God, did not regard equality with God a thing to
be grasped, but emptied Himself, taking the form
of a bond-servant, *and* being made in the like-
ness of men. Being found in appearance as a man,
He humbled Himself by becoming obedient to
the point of death, even death on a cross. For this
reason also, God highly exalted Him, and bestowed
on Him the name which is above every name, so
that at the name of Jesus EVERY KNEE WILL BOW, of
those who are in heaven and on earth and under
the earth, and that every tongue will confess that
Jesus Christ is Lord, to the glory of God the Father.

—PHILIPPIANS 2:5–11 NASB

"A man who can read the New Testament and not
see that Christ claims to be more than a man, can
look all over the sky at high noon on a cloudless
day and not see the sun."

—William E. Biederwolf

Even when Christ ascended into heaven, it was for us. He promised to prepare a place for our arrival at His Father's house . . . He prays for us as our Advocate at His Father's right hand . . . and as He left, He sent the Holy Spirit to be our Counselor, Helper, and constant Companion.

"As the sun can be seen only by its own light, so
Christ can be known only by His own Spirit."

—Robert Leighton

"But when the Father sends the Advocate as my
representative—that is, the Holy Spirit—he will
teach you everything and will remind you of everything I have told you."

—John 14:26 nlt

"Enter into the promises of God. It is your inheritance. You will do more in one year if you are really
filled with the Holy Spirit than you could do in
fifty years apart from Him."

—Smith Wigglesworth

Everyone faces great challenges in life. Some are like potholes in the road, while others stretch before us like bottomless canyons, and seem impossible to overcome. But when Jesus triumphed over death, the grave, and the powers of hell, He brought us along in that victory. Ultimately, in Christ, nothing on earth can defeat us.

> "I don't pray that you may be delivered from your troubles. Instead, I pray that God will give you the strength and patience to bear them."
>
> —Brother Lawrence

> "I have told you all this so that you may have peace in me. Here on earth you will have many trials and sorrows. But take heart, because I have overcome the world."
>
> —John 16:33 nlt

> "I am certain that I never did grow in grace one-half so much anywhere as I have upon the bed of pain."
>
> —Charles Spurgeon

> "Do you think that the infinite God cannot fill and satisfy your heart?"
>
> —François Fénelon

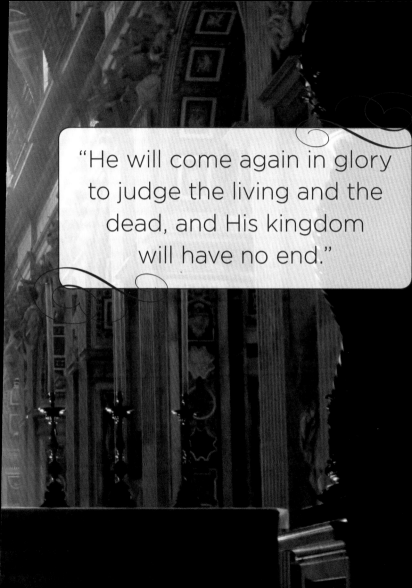

*E*very human organization, government, or kingdom our world has ever known has had its rise and fall, its moment of glory and its inevitable decline. Ruins of once rich and powerful empires litter the world. But the kingdom of Jesus Christ will still be in the morning of its glory when the galaxies have dissolved into dust.

> "Communion with God is the inspiration of life."
>
> —Brooke Foss Westcott

> Then the Lord said to Moses, "Has my arm lost its power? Now you will see whether or not my word comes true!"
>
> —Numbers 11:23 nlt

> *The king's heart is like a stream of water directed by the Lord;*
> *he guides it wherever he pleases.*
>
> —Proverbs 21:1 nlt

He came first as Savior, Redeemer, Example, Healer, Shepherd, Teacher, and the Friend of sinners. When He comes again, He will come as Conqueror and Judge. It is not too late to know the Jesus of that first coming, enabling us to welcome His second coming with joy and anticipation, rather than dread.

> "It is impossible to mentally or socially enslave a Bible-reading people."
>
> —Horace Greeley

As I watched, the Lamb broke the first of the seven seals on the scroll. Then I heard one of the four living beings say with a voice like thunder, "Come!" I looked up and saw a white horse standing there. Its rider carried a bow, and a crown was placed on his head.

—Revelation 6:1–2 nlt

"All heaven and earth resound with that subtle and delicately balanced truth that the old paths are the best paths after all."

—J. C. Ryle

Every day of life has this extra dimension for a believer in Christ: This may be the day when Jesus comes in the clouds and calls me into the sky, into His presence, into the glad company of all who have believed in Him from the beginning of time.

> Then the kings of the earth and the great ones
> and the generals and the rich and the powerful,
> and everyone, slave and free, hid themselves in
> the caves and among the rocks of the mountains,
> calling to the mountains and rocks, "Fall on us and
> hide us from the face of him who is seated on the
> throne, and from the wrath of the Lamb, for the
> great day of their wrath has come, and who can
> stand?"
>
> —REVELATION 6:15–17 ESV

> "Oh, how great peace and quietness would he
> possess who should cut off all vain anxiety and
> place all his confidence in God."
>
> —THOMAS Á KEMPIS

> The LORD says, "I will guide you along
> the best pathway for your life.
>   I will advise you and watch over you."
>
> —PSALM 32:8 NLT

In the eternity to come, we may joyfully travel forever and never cross a border or need a passport. His kingdom will rule over all that ever will be, and as sons and daughters of the King, we will enjoy free passage to every glorious corner of His realm.

> Give yourselves anew to God and to God's service,
> and He will give you the desire and the power to
> open your treasures.
>
> —JOHN ELLERTON

> "You have made them to be a kingdom and priests
> to serve our God, and they will reign on the earth."
> —REVELATION 5:10

> After that comes the end (the completion), when
> He delivers over the kingdom to God the Father
> after rendering inoperative *and* abolishing every
> [other] rule and every authority and power.
> —1 CORINTHIANS 15:24 AMP

> "Men ought to seek with their whole hearts to be
> filled with the Spirit of God. Without being filled
> with the Spirit, it is utterly impossible that an indi-
> vidual Christian or a church can ever live or work
> as God desires."
>
> —ANDREW MURRAY

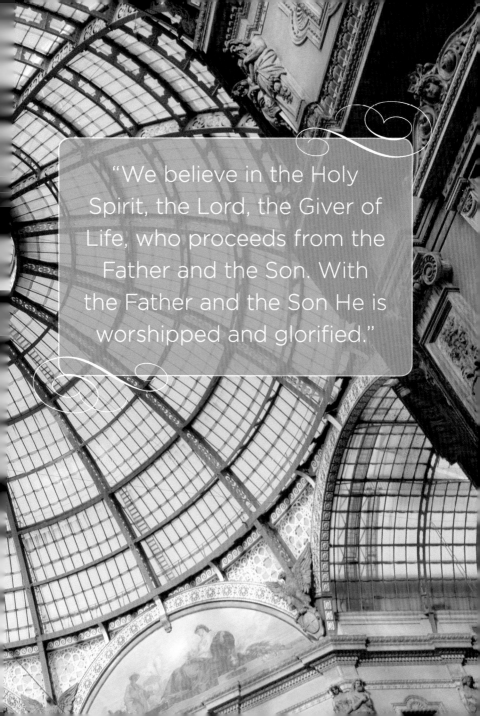

"We believe in the Holy Spirit, the Lord, the Giver of Life, who proceeds from the Father and the Son. With the Father and the Son He is worshipped and glorified."

Why would Jesus tell His grieving disciples in John 16:7 that it would be "for your good that I am going away"? What could possibly be better than the physical presence of Jesus Himself? The answer is that He would send the Holy Spirit, who is not only *with* every believer in all the world for all time, but actually resident *within* every believer. To this day, He is a gift beyond any measure of value.

> "I seek the will of the Spirit of God through or in connection with the Word of God. The Spirit and the Word must be combined. If I look to the Spirit alone without the Word, I lay myself open to great delusions also."
>
> —George Mueller

> It is God who enables us . . . to stand firm for Christ. He has commissioned us, and he has identified us as his own by placing the Holy Spirit in our hearts as the first installment that guarantees everything he has promised us.
>
> —2 Corinthians 1:21–22 nlt

> "As the sun can be seen only by its own light, so Christ can be known only by His own Spirit."
>
> —Robert Leighton

In those times when we feel overwhelmed, discouraged, and alone, hardly knowing what to pray, the Holy Spirit steps in to carry our ragged, disconnected thoughts and sighs, translating them into powerful prayers that He presents to the Father.

"It is in vain for man to endeavor to instruct man in those things which the Holy Spirit alone can teach."

—Madame Guyon

"But the Helper, the Holy Spirit, whom the Father will send in my name, he will teach you all things and bring to your remembrance all that I have said to you."

—John 14:26 ESV

"Destitute of the Fire of God, nothing else counts; possessing Fire, nothing else matters."

—Samuel Chadwick

The Holy Spirit is not an "It." He is a living Person, equal to the Father and the Son. He is not only our Comforter and Advocate during these sometimes turbulent days of life on earth, He will be our close Companion and Friend through all eternity.

"Sometimes, the Spirit desires to slow us down and lead us into silence. Our society is addicted to noise, and for that reason we are often insensitive to the Spirit of God."

—Unknown

"Whoever believes in me, as the Scripture has said, 'Out of his heart will flow rivers of living water.'"

—John 7:38 ESV

"Spirit filled souls are ablaze for God. They love with a love that glows. They serve with a faith that kindles. They serve with a devotion that consumes. They hate sin with fierceness that burns. They rejoice with a joy that radiates. Love is perfected in the fire of God."

—SAMUEL CHADWICK

When anxiety closes in or when we feel paralyzed by indecision and don't know which way to go, the Holy Spirit will be our Guide and lead us "turn by turn" to a place of refuge and safety. As the prophet foretold in Isaiah 30:21: "Whether you turn to the right or to the left, your ears will hear a voice behind you, saying, 'This is the way; walk in it.'"

"For the Holy Spirit will teach you at that time what needs to be said."

—LUKE 12:12 NLT

"Salt, when dissolved in water, may disappear, but it does not cease to exist. We can be sure of its presence by tasting the water. Likewise, the indwelling Christ, though unseen, will be made evident to others from the love which he imparts to us."

—SADHU SUNDAR SINGH

"I believe that I cannot come to my Lord Jesus Christ by my own intelligence or power. But the Holy Spirit called me by the Gospel, enlightened me with his gifts, made me holy and kept me in the true faith, just as she calls, gathers together, enlightens and makes holy the whole Church on earth and keeps it with Jesus in the one, true faith."

—MARTIN LUTHER

"The Bible was not given for our information but for our transformation."

—D. L. MOODY

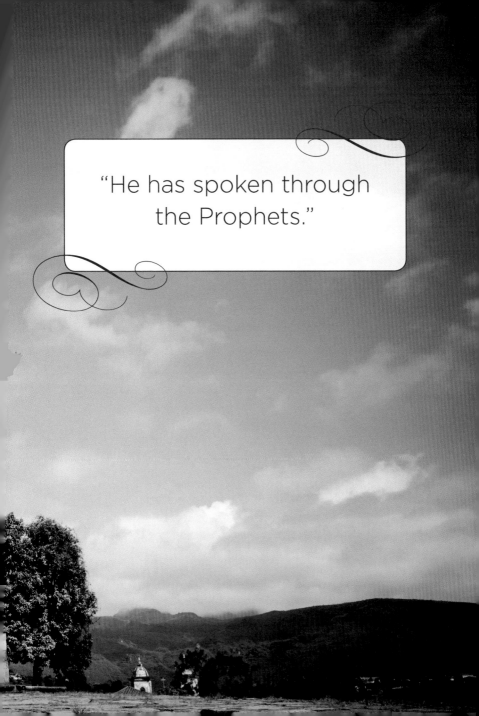

"He has spoken through the Prophets."

In earlier days, many godly men and women longed to hear from God, but had to wait—sometimes months or long years—before word would filter down from one of the Lord's prophets. Today the Holy Spirit directly speaks to people from the pages of the Bible. He takes the eternal truths of Scripture and applies them directly to our current needs, questions, and problems.

> "He is the one all the prophets testified about, saying that everyone who believes in him will have their sins forgiven through his name."
>
> —Acts 10:43 NLT

> "He who kneels the most, stands the best."
>
> —D. L. Moody

"The Word of God is the fulcrum upon which the
lever of prayer is placed, and by which things are
mightily moved."

—E. M. Bounds

We have a God who speaks. He has spoken through His
prophets . . . through His Son . . . through His apostles . . . through
the authors of the Bible . . . and through Spirit-filled brothers and
sisters in Christ. Sometimes, He also chooses to speak through our
circumstances—even the ones that break our hearts. As Jesus often
said, "He who has ears to hear, let him hear."

"Not only do we not know God except through
Jesus Christ; We do not even know ourselves except
through Jesus Christ."

—Blaise Pascal

"And if you are not faithful with other people's
things, why should you be trusted with things
of your own? No one can serve two masters. For
you will hate one and love the other; you will be
devoted to one and despise the other. You cannot
serve both God and money."

—Luke 16:12–13 nlt

"It is impossible for that man to despair who
remembers that his Helper is omnipotent."

—Jeremy Taylor

He has spoken warnings, clear and unmistakable as the pealing of a great iron bell. He has spoken words of wisdom and counsel, showing the path ahead in bright sunlight, or as illumined by a lantern in the dark. He has spoken words of love, in poetry and song, in story and drama, in long, thoughtful letters, and in sudden, dramatic revelations of the future.

> *"For God speaks in one way,*
> *and in two, though man does not perceive it."*
> —JOB 33:14 ESV

> "In order to the existence of such a ministry in the
> Church, there is requisite an authority received
> from God, and consequently power and knowledge
> imparted from God for the exercise of such minis-
> try; and where a man possesses these, although the
> bishop has not laid hands upon him according to
> his traditions, God has Himself appointed him."
> —JOHN WYCLIFFE

He speaks . . . but have we heard? Are we listening? To Elijah, the Spirit spoke in a "still small voice" (1 Kings 19:12 KJV). Sometimes He still does. It's a voice that can easily be drowned out by the noise of our surroundings or the anxiety and confusion of our distracted, overloaded lives. Even so, God's Spirit continues to speak, to this very day, and those who want to hear Him most will hear Him.

> "Let our Lord's sweet hand . . . make us stones and
> pillars in His Father's House."
> —SAMUEL RUTHERFORD

"The Bible is alive; it speaks to me.
It has feet; it runs after me.
It has hands; it lays hold of me!"

—Martin Luther

"Keep this Book of the Law always on your lips; meditate on it day and night, so that you may be careful to do everything written in it. Then you will be prosperous and successful."

—Joshua 1:8

"The Scriptures teach us the best way of living, the noblest way of suffering and the most comfortable way of dying."

—John Flavel

"We believe in one holy catholic and apostolic Church."

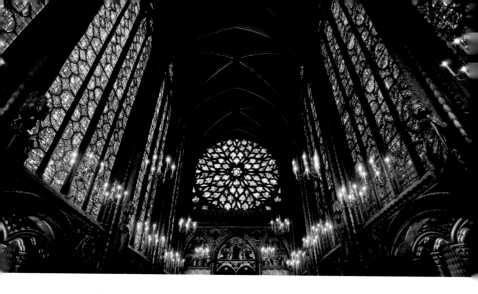

*T*he church of Jesus Christ is a flowering, fruit-bearing tree with roots two thousand years deep and branches reaching into every nation on earth.

> " . . . We make our own the profession of the
> faith that we carry in our heart . . . We have the
> catholic faith in the creed, known to the faithful
> and committed to memory, contained in a form of
> expression as concise as has been rendered admissible by the circumstances."
>
> —AUGUSTINE

> For as in one body we have many members, and
> the members do not all have the same function,
> so we, though many, are one body in Christ, and
> individually members one of another.
>
> —ROMANS 12:4–5 ESV

"Here am I, send me; send me to the ends of the
earth; send me to the rough, the savage pagans
of the wilderness; send me from all that is called
comfort on earth; send me even to death itself,
if it be but in Your service, and to promote Your
kingdom."

—David Brainerd

Here is a wonder: As followers of Christ we may encounter a
brother or sister in the Lord living on the opposite side of the earth,
speaking another language, steeped in a radically different culture—
and immediately have a bond greater than with a nonbelieving
neighbor who has lived next door to us for a decade.

Be devoted to one another in love. Honor one
another above yourselves. Never be lacking in zeal,
but keep your spiritual fervor, serving the Lord.

—Romans 12:10–11

"The Bible knows nothing of solitary religion."

—John Wesley

"The church of Christ is the multitude of all those
who believe in Christ for the remission of sins,
and who are thankful for that mercy and who love
the law of God purely, and who hate the sin in this
world and long for the life to come."

—William Tyndale

The Church of Jesus Christ comprises not only those who at this moment believe across the globe, but all of those who have ever placed faith in Jesus through the centuries and millennia. In heaven, the distinctions of when and where and how long we lived on earth will melt away as we love and serve one another as a loving extended family.

> "We are a long time in learning that all our strength and salvation is in God."
> —DAVID BRAINERD

> "One family, we dwell in Him,
> One church above, beneath,
> Though now divided by the stream,
> The narrow stream of death."
> —CHARLES WESLEY

> For the Lord himself will come down from heaven with a commanding shout, with the voice of the archangel, and with the trumpet call of God. First, the Christians who have died will rise from their graves.
> —1 THESSALONIANS 4:16 NLT

Ideas, styles, attitudes, priorities, trends, fashions, and technologies change continually. Even the map of the world is a moving, transient thing, with nations rising and receding, proud empires swelling then dwindling into dust. Through it all, across the millennia, the core and essential teachings of Christ's apostles have remained constant as a mountain range, changeless as the great constellations.

For you know that God paid a ransom to save you from the empty life you inherited from your ancestors. And the ransom he paid was not mere gold or silver. It was the precious blood of Christ, the sinless, spotless Lamb of God.

—1 Peter 1:18–19 nlt

"If works and love do not blossom forth, it is not genuine faith, the gospel has not yet gained a foothold, and Christ is not yet rightly known."

—Martin Luther

Let us think of ways to motivate one another to acts of love and good works. And let us not neglect our meeting together, as some people do, but encourage one another, especially now that the day of his return is drawing near.

—Hebrews 10:24–25 nlt

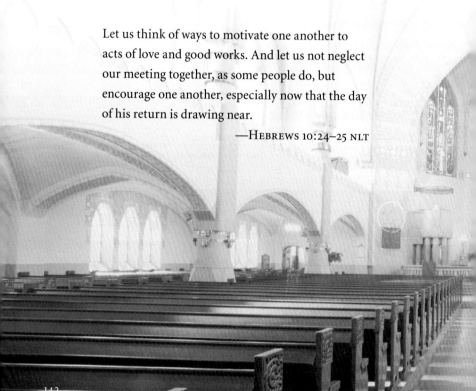

We want to work together with you so you will be
full of joy, for it is by your own faith that you stand
firm.

—2 Corinthians 1:24 nlt

"The church where worship rises to God's ear
is that, and that only, where the soul ascends.
No matter whether it be gathered in cathedral
or barn; whether it sit in silence or send up a
hymn; whether the minister speak from care-
fully prepared notes, or from immediate, fervent,
irrepressible suggestion. If God be loved, and Jesus
Christ be welcomed to the soul, and his instruc-
tions be meekly and wisely heard, and the solemn
purpose grow up to do all duty amidst all conflict,
sacrifice, and temptation, then the true end of the
church is answered."

—William E. Channing

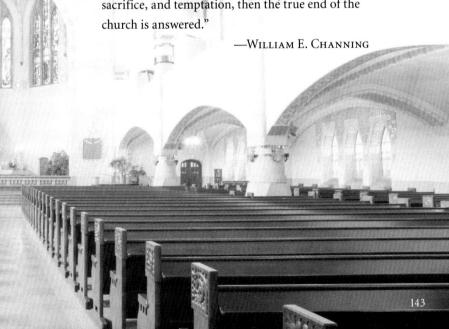

"We acknowledge one baptism for the forgiveness of sins."

*W*hen Philip baptized the Ethiopian official in a small lake off of the Highway to Africa, there were no other human eyes to witness the act . . . yet it is still something we talk about after twenty centuries of world history. Baptism may be a symbol, but it is one that shapes destinies.

> "Therefore, go and make disciples of all the nations, baptizing them in the name of the Father and the Son and the Holy Spirit."
>
> —MATTHEW 28:19 NLT

> "When you become satisfied with God, however, everything else so loses its charm that He can give it to you without harm."
>
> —A. B. SIMPSON

> "Because God has made us for Himself, our hearts are restless until they rest in Him."
>
> —AUGUSTINE

Baptism paints a picture for the eyes of people and angels. The scene it depicts is nothing less than death and rebirth, of laying down an old life and embracing a new.

> ". . . Each gift will be welcomed by Him who gave Himself for us all, and who asks in return for ourselves as a living sacrifice to Him."
>
> —JOHN ELLERTON

"If you'll hold on to me for dear life," says GOD,
  "I'll get you out of any trouble.
I'll give you the best of care
  if you'll only get to know and trust me.
Call me and I'll answer, be at your side in bad times;
  I'll rescue you, then throw you a party.
I'll give you a long life,
  give you a long drink of salvation!"

—PSALM 91:14–16 MSG

When we are baptized, someone else does it to us for us; we can't baptize ourselves. In the same way, salvation is something Someone has accomplished for us, and the only way we can participate in the process is by submitting to it.

"Behold, how happy is the man whom God reproves,
So do not despise the discipline of the Almighty."

—JOB 5:17 NASB

"Our Lord and Master Jesus Christ, in saying,
Repent Ye, intended that the whole of the life of
believers should be repentance."

—MARTIN LUTHER

"Cease striving and know that I am God;
I will be exalted among the nations, I will be exalted in
  the earth."

—PSALM 46:10 NASB

We are all linked, not by our good and praiseworthy qualities, but by our sins before a holy God, and our radical need for grace and forgiveness. In baptism we confess publicly what we have already admitted quietly to the Lord and to ourselves: We are hopelessly and eternally lost apart from the saving, cleansing, restoring power of Jesus Christ, and the blood He spilled on the cross for our sins.

> "There is one case of death-bed repentance recorded, that of the penitent thief, that none should despair; and only one that none should presume."
>
> —AUGUSTINE

> When Jesus had tasted it, he said, "It is finished!" Then he bowed his head and released his spirit.
>
> —JOHN 19:30 NLT

> "If Christ has died for me—ungodly as I am, without strength as I am—then I can no longer live in sin, but must arouse myself to love and serve Him who has redeemed me. I cannot trifle with the evil that killed my best Friend. I must be holy for his sake. How can I live in sin when He has died to save me from it?"
>
> —CHARLES SPURGEON

> "The glory is not in the task, but in the doing it for Him."
>
> —JEAN INGELOW

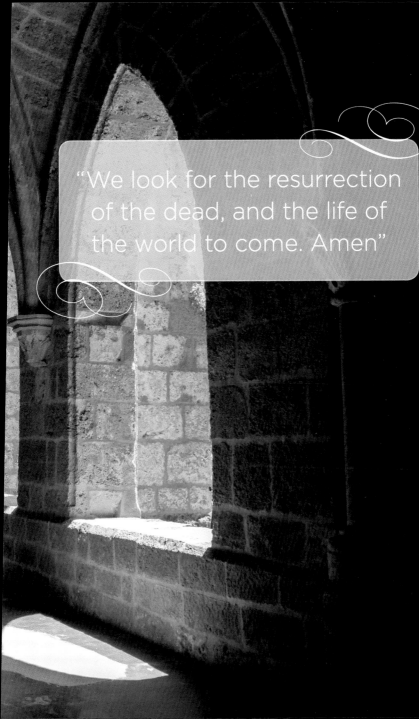

"We look for the resurrection of the dead, and the life of the world to come. Amen"

*S*o much of what believers in Christ hold true flies in the face of the strictly natural point of view. Death is not final, time itself is temporary, and good-byes on earth really mean "see you later, in our Father's house."

> *"How strange this fear of death is!*
> *We are never frightened at a sunset."*
>
> —George MacDonald

> We proclaim to you the one who existed from the beginning, whom we have heard and seen. We saw him with our own eyes and touched him with our own hands. He is the Word of life.
>
> —1 John 1:1 nlt

> "We will never know perfection this side of eternity."
>
> —Unknown

The Bible tells us enough about heaven to intrigue us, delight us, comfort us, and motivate us, but leaves enough unsaid that we have to exercise both faith and imagination to think about our future home. And thinking such thoughts is exactly what the Bible says we should do: "Think about the things of heaven, not the things of earth" (Colossians 3:2 nlt).

[Fix your] eyes on Jesus, the author and perfecter of faith, who for the joy set before Him endured the cross, despising the shame, and has sat down at the right hand of the throne of God.

—Hebrews 12:2 NASB

"It is prosperity that we cannot endure."

—Martin Luther

"The principal act of courage is to endure and withstand dangers doggedly rather than to attack them."

—Thomas Aquinas

Everyone truly alive is looking for something, watching the horizon for some sign or indication of diversion, hope, peace, relief, provision, healing, or love. We who have placed our full hope in Christ look for the same things as everyone else—but we also lift our gaze higher than the usual earth-centered hopes and desires. We know there will be life beyond life, reunion beyond separation, and comfort that will outweigh all of our pains, disappointments, and sorrows.

"Turn your eyes upon Jesus,
Look full in His wonderful face,
And the things of earth will grow strangely dim,
In the light of His glory and grace."

—Helen Howarth Lemmel

The Lord will fight for you,
and you shall hold your peace and remain at rest.

—Exodus 14:14 AMP

"Not till we are ready to throw our very life's love into the troublesome little things can we be really faithful in that which is least and faithful also in much."

—James Reed

Memories of loved ones who have already left this earth for heaven may fade with the passing of time. But the persons themselves have not in any sense "faded." In fact, they are more alive, more in-focus, more complete, and more filled with life and personality and purpose than we ever knew them to be on earth. It's like the difference between an old, faded black-and-white photo and full-color, high-definition 3-D.

We don't yet see things clearly. We're squinting in a fog, peering through a mist. But it won't be long before the weather clears and the sun shines bright! We'll see it all then, see it all as clearly as God sees us, knowing him directly just as he knows us!

—1 Corinthians 13:12 MSG

"Christ is not valued at all unless He be valued above all."

—Augustine

"We ought to see the face of God every morning before we see the face of man."

—D. L. Moody